West Chicago Public Library District
118 West Washington
West Chicago, IL 60185-2803
Phone # (630) 231-1552
Fax # (630) 231-1709

Marine Mammals

Orcas

by Jody Sullivan Rake

Consulting editor: Gail Saunders-Smith, PhD

CAPSTONE PRESS
a capstone imprint

Pebble Plus is published by Capstone Publishers,
1710 Roe Crest Drive, North Mankato, MN 56003
www.capstonepub.com

Library of Congress Cataloging-in-Publication Data
Rake, Jody Sullivan.
Orcas / by Jody Sullivan Rake.
p. cm.—(Pebble plus. Marine mammals)
Includes bibliographical references and index.
Summary: "Simple text and full-color photographs provide a brief introduction to orcas"—Provided by publisher.
ISBN 978-1-4296-8717-1 (library binding)
ISBN 978-1-62065-313-5 (Ebook PDF)
1. Killer whale—Juvenile literature. I. Title.

QL737.C432R358 2013
599.53'6—dc23   2012002628

Editorial Credits
Jeni Wittrock, editor; Ted Williams, designer; Svetlana Zhurkin, media researcher; Kathy McColley,
production specialist

Photo Credits
Alamy: Juniors Bildarchiv, 19, WaterFrame, 15; Dreamstime: Ivkovich, 21, Karoline Cullen, 13, Rinus Baak, 7; National
Geographic Stock: Ralph Lee Hopkins, 11; Newscom: Danita Delimont Photography/Jon Cornforth, 5; SeaPics: Ingrid
Visser, cover; Shutterstock: CampCrazy Photography, 17, mcherevan (splash), cover, 1, Mikhail Dudarev (water texture),
cover, 1, Miles Away Photography, 9, Tom Middleton, 3, Yulia Mansurova (orca), 8

Note to Parents and Teachers

The Marine Mammals series supports national science standards related to life science. This
book describes and illustrates orcas. The images support early readers in understanding the
text. The repetition of words and phrases helps early readers learn new words. This book
also introduces early readers to subject-specific vocabulary words, which are defined in the
Glossary section. Early readers may need assistance to read some words and to use the Table of
Contents, Glossary, Read More, Internet Sites, and Index sections of the book.

Printed in the United States of America in North Mankato, Minnesota.
042012   006682CGF12

Table of Contents

Cruising the Waves

Speedy orcas cruise through the ocean waves. These marine mammals are sometimes called killer whales.

Orcas feel at home
in cold ocean water.
Most orcas live in the Arctic
and Antarctic Oceans.

Orca Range

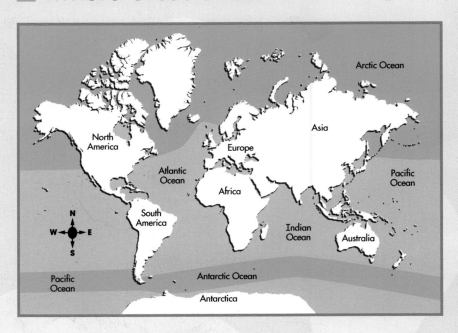

where orcas swim

An Orca's Body

Male orcas weigh
up to 12,000 pounds
(5,400 kilograms).
Females are smaller.

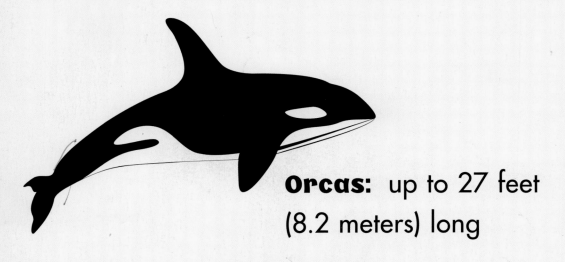

Orcas: up to 27 feet
(8.2 meters) long

 5 feet (1.5 m) long

Orcas' smooth, rubbery
skin is black and white.
A thick layer of fat
called blubber
keeps orcas warm.

Orcas have blowholes
on top of their heads
to help them breathe.
Under water, an orca's
blowhole closes tightly.

Top Predators

Orcas are top predators in the ocean. They eat fish, seals, and otters. Orcas even eat other whales and dolphins!

Orcas have sharp teeth
for grabbing their prey.
Their top and bottom
teeth fit together
like a zipper.

Orca Life Cycle

Female orcas have one baby,
or calf, at a time. Mothers feed
their babies for about one year.
Then the calves can hunt
on their own.

Orcas live in groups called pods. The pods swim and hunt together. Orcas live 30 to 35 years.

Glossary

blowhole—a hole on the top of an orca's head; orcas breathe air through blowholes

blubber— a thick layer of fat under the skin of some animals; blubber keeps orcas warm

calf—a young orca

mammal—a warm-blooded animal that breathes air; mammals have hair or fur; female mammals feed milk to their young

marine—living in salt water

pod—a group of orcas

predator—an animal that hunts other animals for food

prey—an animal hunted by another animal for food

Read More

Armour, Michael C. *Orca Song.* Smithsonian Oceanic Collection. Norwalk, Conn.: Soundprints, 2011.

Lunis, Natalie. *Killer Whale: The World's Largest Dolphin.* More Supersized! New York: Bearport Pub., 2010.

Rake, Jody Sullivan. *Bottlenose Dolphins.* Marine Mammals. Mankato, Minn.: Capstone Press, 2012.

Internet Sites

FactHound offers a safe, fun way to find Internet sites related to this book. All of the sites on FactHound have been researched by our staff.

Here's all you do:

Visit *www.facthound.com*

Type in this code: 9781429687171

Check out projects, games and lots more at
www.capstonekids.com

Index

Word Count: 163
Grade: 1
Early-Intervention Level: 15